What's an Abortion, Anyway?

Carly Manes ✳ Emulsify

Printed in China

ISBN: 978-0-578-89924-4
Library of Congress Control Number: 2021911592

This book is meant to be a resource for young people who are curious about abortion or have someone in their life who has had an abortion. We chose each and every word with intention, and want to share a few notes about language before you dive in.

This book was written with the assumption that the person reading has a basic understanding of how pregnancy happens. There are many fantastic books that help explain the fundamentals of reproduction and pregnancy. We recommend *What Makes a Baby* by Cory Silverberg if you're looking for such a resource.

Folks of all different gender identities get pregnant, meaning that folks of all different gender identities have abortions. It was important to us that this book honors everyone who has abortions and challenges the mainstream social assumption that only cisgender women have abortions. The beautiful thing about language is that it's forever evolving and changing. The words we use in this book were the most fitting at the time of publication.

This book is dedicated to anyone who has ever had or will ever have an abortion(s).

We want to thank our friends, family, and community members who read the many draft iterations of this book and provided critical feedback. We also want to thank all of the We Testify storytellers and Dr. Jamila Perritt who graciously shared their images with us for this book.

When a person gets pregnant, many different things can happen.

Some people are pregnant for many months and have a baby. That's what happened with you!

Some people have a miscarriage.

A miscarriage is when a pregnancy isn't healthy enough to keep growing.

Some people have an abortion.

An abortion is when someone decides
to stop growing their pregnancy.

There are many different ways that people who are pregnant can have an abortion.

Some people see a doctor who does a special procedure to remove the pregnancy from inside a person's body.

Other people take medicine to stop the pregnancy from growing bigger.

Abortion is very safe and millions of people have abortions every year all around the world.

No matter how someone has an abortion, everyone should be able to decide the way that is best for them.

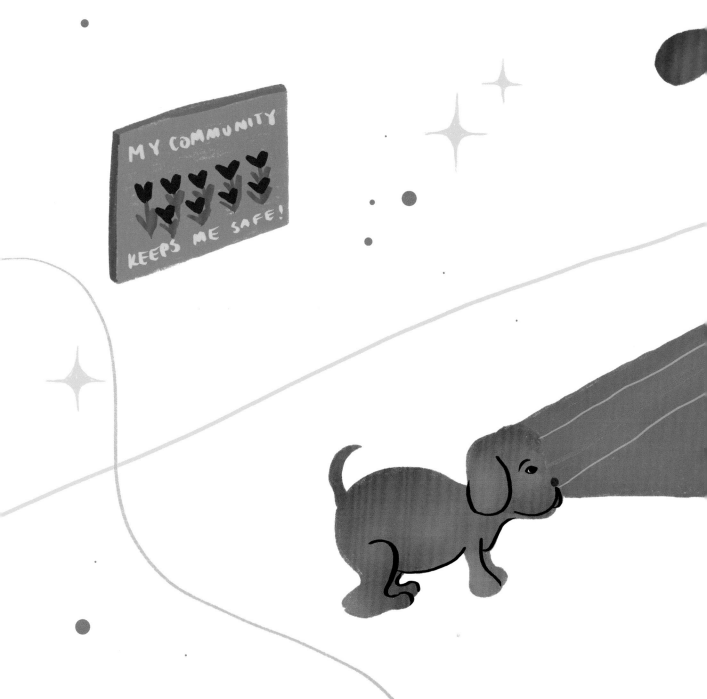

People have abortions for different reasons.

Some people have abortions because they like their family exactly as it is.

Some people have abortions because they can't take care of a new baby right now.

Some people have abortions because their doctors say pregnancy could make them sick.

No matter the reason, everyone should be able to make this decision for themselves.

People have many different feelings before, during, and after their abortion.

Some people want to talk about it, and some people don't.

Some people feel happy or calm.

Some people feel sad or lonely.

Many people feel all of these things at the same time.

No matter how someone feels about their abortion, they deserve to be treated with love and respect.

We can never really know what it is like to be someone else.

About the Author

Carly Manes (she/her) is a white, queer, Jewish full-spectrum doula from New York. She has always believed that young people deserve transparency when it comes to information about their sexual health and bodies. Carly has been a practicing abortion doula for over six years, supporting more than 2,000 individuals during their in-clinic procedures. She loves the beach, chicken tenders, and her communities. She lives with her partner Mo and their playful pitbull Mickey.

About the Illustrator

Mar (they/them) is a brown genderqueer cultural worker and abortion doula. Under the name Emulsify, they create art that helps them heal, learn, advocate, and imagine new worlds. They believe all art is powerful and political. M lives in Brooklyn with their wife and spends a lot of time creating while snuggling their cat and pups. Through their work, M has made incredible friendships, learned from brilliant peers, and found their home.